The Way,
The Truth,
&
The Life

A book of inspirations through spiritual poetry

Angelicia Roberts

The Way, The Truth, & The Life

ISBN: 0-9746936-3-4

Cover Design: Amy Schneider, Evil Genius Design
Cover Photo: ProEx
Printing: Bookmobile
Bindery: Midwest Editions

In loving memory of:
Mother Mary Harmon
&
My grandparents,
Phillip & Ollie Hill

To mom and the rest of my family: You are my first and biggest fans who believed in me and my God-given potential even before I learned to. You keep me grounded (in love). Thank you for your sacrifices, patience and support.

To the reader: These words were carefully crafted in love to assure you of the significance of your life in God's eyes. And to show you that no matter where you are, you're not too far away for God to demonstrate His love and His realness.

Father God,

I thank you for entrusting me with this assignment to bring to pass. For taking the time to show yourself to me, it has helped bring so many things in perspective and has given me a sense of purpose, direction and inner strength that only you can provide. I just want to say I appreciate you for that. In Jesus name, Amen.

Daughter Arise

For I called you in such a time as this
A time to bloom, a time to shine
To be all that I called you to be

For it took some time and thought
to make and form your being
I have formed you in my Excellence
I have formed you in my Gloriousness
For I have made you Fearlessly and Wonderfully
Count it all joy, in your existence
For at this hour, you'll meet my face
And because you were made in my image
you will be ready to take flight
Your next stop is Destiny
No time for regrets or to regress
I've removed all of life's pests
I've cleansed you from all unrighteousness
I have made you whole
You can search, but you won't find
a "complete" definition of you
My Beautiful Daughter Arise
It's your season, it's time
You're anointed, in my time for you to shine
Open up your heart
The metamorphism of your soul butterfly is complete
You are free
You are free
From all of your iniquities and infirmities
Your past can no longer disturb your peace
Your joy won't fade through adversities
Let your freedom ring
Set the captives free
Grace and Glory will shine in your testimony
There is power in your testimony
My Daughter Arise
And be encouraged in such a time
Be encouraged at all times

Know that you know that I got you,
that I'm with you, that I love you
Everything you need, I've already provided
All you have to do is open yourself up
to believe and receive
No more condemnation, no more hindering
Speak love and only light to yourself,
to your sisters, to your family
For the I Am that I Am
has made you whole
With nothing broken, missing or lacking
You are exactly where I want you to be
It's a time to bloom, a time to shine
No need to compromise
You just be You
And daughter, please, Arise.

Table of Contents

Introduction: Experiencing God in the process of a purposeful life 11

Chapter One: He Loves Me 13
Personal Reflection 15
An Empty Place 17
Never will I leave you; never will I forsake you 19
A Purposeful Life 21
A Higher Cause 24
He Loves Me 26
Foundational Prayer 28

Chapter Two: Trusting the Process 29
Personal Reflection 31
The Process of a Purposeful Life 33
In the Meantime 35
Things aren't always what they seem 37
Leaning to Own Understanding 39
Put Your Trust in Me 41
Trusting Prayer 43

Chapter Three: Experiencing God 45
Personal Reflection 47
Experiencing God 49
To Him the Glory 51
Consecration 52
Remain in Me 54
Is it meant to be meant for me? 56
Prayer of Excellence 58

Chapter Four: Two-Steppin' with God.. 59

Personal Reflection.. 61

Even though: Psalms 23:4 63

Resting Tempo.. 64

Receive the Peace.. 65

Living a Victorious Life 68

Two-Steppin' with God 70

Guidance Prayer 71

Scripture Notes.. 72

References... 75

Appreciation page 76

Special Tribute: Daily 77

Introduction
Experiencing God in the Process of a Purposeful Life

In the process of writing The Way, The Truth & The Life, I was really struggling with the introduction. I was looking at outside sources: other books, dictionaries, my mentor and editor, etc. It wasn't until I stopped looking outside for the answer to look within that the intro began to flow. Even as I thought about, the whole concept, as human beings we tend to look outward or externally at times for answers that only we ourselves can give. We look in all the wrong places, and when we're not looking what we need is revealed to us. It's like God's saying, "look no further, I have given you everything you need, I am all that you need." Through my own experiences with Him, I find that my perspective continues to change.

In the book *Experiencing God* by Henry T. Blackaby and Claude V. King, it talks about, no one has a natural desire after the things of God; not until he or she clearly identifies God's hand in their life. I personally didn't have an agenda or a target market of who this book is for. I know that some people will get this book because they love me, and want to support and invest in me. Apart from this small cluster of friends and family, I really believe that the ones who are drawn to get this book are the ones that God is at work in their lives–even before one recognizes or acknowledges it. It's an individual experience, and it's between the reader and God what may resonate with them.

This book is broken up into four chapters: He Loves Me, Trusting the Process, Experiencing God and Two-Steppin' With God. Each chapter begins with a personal reflection, which is a summary of my own experience with the subject, and it sets the tone of what to expect in content for the chapter. Each chapter ends with a prayer for the reader to use if (s)/he desires to (with the understanding that I'm already in agreement and believing with him/her).

This book is about faith, hope, love and foundation. This entire book is about an intimate companionship with God. This companionship is an influence for individuals constantly evolving into being all they were created to be. It's a continuum, an on-going process, and a journey, of experiencing God in the process of a purposeful life. Trusting God to orchestrate and to be the architect of our lives no matter what we face on the journey. Trusting Him to accomplish what He had in mind when we were conceived. It's a lifetime journey of experiences of coming to know Him as the Way, the Truth and the Life.

CHAPTER ONE:

He Loves Me

Personal Reflection: He Loves Me

Love. Love is the key. I learned that I couldn't love others until I learned to love myself. I really didn't learn to love myself until I understood how God loved me first.[1] I had to strip away other people's thoughts, societal views and even my own opinions on why I was worthy, in order to embrace a more solid, spiritual foundation that is called God-esteem. I then began to see how God is love and His nature is love.[2] He is constantly working on my behalf, because He loves me. He keeps me, gives me guidance, provides for me and protects (in ways that I'm still recognizing) on the daily basis in order to fulfill His purpose through me.

It has definitely been a process to not rely on other people, or things to give me fulfillment, value[3] and a sense of purpose.[4] Or even to fill a void or emptiness in me. In the midst I was trying to be there for other people when I needed to save myself. Relying on people and things was definitely a loss, because I was never satisfied or happy within myself. I was driving people crazy because they could never please me. It wasn't until I really understood the love of God that I learned that all that I am and could ever hope to be is[5] rooted in Him. Rooted in God is being rooted in love. As I continually experience this love it has given me a message of hope, a persuasion of comfort and assurance that I'm not alone in this world and that God loves me and has been with me the entire time. God cares about my life and my existence more than anyone can imagine,[6] my life was thought of and pre-destined. It's the same thing for you. As He has this to show me, I wanted to show others.

Even in times of loneliness, when I have felt inadequate or displaced, when I questioned if God was really there. I have to remember that in every step and process or transition in life that I enter, no matter what–I can count on God to be with me.[7] As I made that connection with God and acknowledged Him in my life my whole perception has changed in how I view myself, how I view others around me, how I view my life, how I view things that I went through and where I believe I am going. God is love. In God love is my foundation and motivation. My focus and my priorities has changed. As He continues to bless me and manifest His love and favor upon me more and more I want to give to others what He has freely given to me. Since I have this confidence in the love God has for me, I now strive to be all I can be, that I might represent Him, using what He has given me to bless others. It's hard to say that I am competent in God's love when I'm having a hard time loving myself, or the ones right in front of me. It's still a daily process to make the decision to love in spite of, to keep a smile on my face. Love is the key, because God is love and He is the answer.

I now really believe that the things that I went through were to help some-one else through. If it wasn't for God's love, seeing something valuable in me, I don't believe that I would be here. It's amazing to me when I consider how much I would have missed, and what others would have missed if I wasn't here, available for God to use me. The greatness of God's love is unspeakable. I believe my pur-pose is to serve God, which is done through my encounters with people. I believe everything I do is being done to Him and whatever I do affects more people than what I realize. It's all about representing Him, allowing Him to use us. That's what it's all about. It all boils down to Him, to love,[8] and being rooted in fact that, there is nothing to fear.[9]

AN EMPTY PLACE

How is your happiness defined when, all that you ever hoped for is gone? Meeting disappointments again, and again, because you can't even reach your own expectations. And you're experiencing frustration. Blaming the Creator, even in knowing He has given you a free will to do what you please. Blaming your past, history, and life in your decision to remain in a state of slavery. Blaming society that you chose not to help change what you don't like seeing. The person you most depend upon is gone or you just can't any more rely on. Needing someone to talk to and it seems like for you, no one is there. Nobody cares. You're feeling remorse because you haven't gained reciprocity.

And you feel that gives you the right to act a fool. Internally, you keep asking and searching. What do you do when you've done all that you could do, to help yourself or someone else? You're realizing your limitations, experiencing a lot of haste and just don't know where you're going. Living beyond your means and yourself, overextending.

Not even being honest with yourself, let alone someone else, about who you really are. Wasting time and energy because the fuel you're running is on "E". Trying to fill emptiness inside you that only God can do. So you feed yourself with worldly folly, a taste of bliss to have your release. And all you're asking for is a release, to be relieved of all this pain and insanity. A peace of mind, you're in reach for serenity. You can't even process prosperity and in life succeeding because of your own mess. Rejection is validated with feelings of worthlessness and ugliness.

You're just trying to survive, to stay alive. Taking defense to the world because you feel it has plotted against you. And you feel you have the right to feel the way you do. So you act out towards everything. And all you're in need of is some tender loving. This space inside you is an empty place. A dry place that you're not able to on your own cultivate. In your eyes of abandonment, you're blind to the beauty of God's grace in this deserted place. The vehicle you depended on to take you where you need to be. The vehicle you felt defined you and your life meaning, turned out not to be what you were expecting. Not realizing the divine fuel, as you play the same old tune, and in your mind, your entire past you play through. Not noticing the role God has played in the same place that has been keeping you sane. He has always provided a light. He has been the light. He has always provided an escape from anything involved with your internal agony and suffering. It involves you accepting the invitation and moving. Because He won't overrule the free will He's given you. In focusing on the wrong placements in your life, you have already missed what gives you fulfillment, and what has been right. You're now learning to exceed your feelings in order to speak and walk in the light on everything. What you've been searching for, depending on, God has inside you placed. You're learning to believe in you and increasing your faith. No more allowing your emotions drive you to the grave. To whatever blues you might play, God will sing away. When you're feeling unloved, or feeling you just can't make it or go on. When you're experiencing more confusion than clarity. When you're scared and worried and it doesn't feel like any-body can relate. Feeling alone. When you're feeling that your money, your worth is gone. Feeling inadequate, insufficient and insignificant, all because what around you is going on.

If no one else validates you, your life is not a mistake. Learning to affirm when no one else will, that you are okay. When no one or nothing else will give you a compliment. You have to recognize your own comeliness, and what makes you complete. You are one of God's masterpieces. He will trade your ashes in return for beauty. You will find that nothing or no one else can fill this empty place. And you will see the beauty of God's grace in that deserted place.

"...Never will I leave you; never will I forsake you."

He says
He'll never leave
nor forsake me

And I question
what He really means
trying to obtain
an understanding

Revealing to my heart
to fill with peace
Never will He leave
nor forsake

And I'm wondering
how can this be
when I stand
in the midst
of comfortless misery

With no shoulders to lean on
and my tears are fluid
and my heart heavy
I've grown weary

Never will He leave
nor forsake me

How about
when my account is empty
and the doors are closing
when I feel no one understands
or accepts me for me

He says 'look to me'
that He'll never forsake
He'll never leave

In rhythm with my heart
He says He's in sync
He is in
every breath
I breathe
That is how close
He is to me

As I miss my blessings
by trying to
forward wind the lessons
and me,
He's just testing

He says
He'll never leave
nor forsake me

A spiritual awakening
where He has me
is where I need to be

And nothing and no one
is greater than He
than His ability

Before He was thinking
of times like these
He said that
they aren't meant to harm me
but brighten
what lies ahead of me

Decision making
to remain in
what He's telling me
Never will He leave
nor forsake me

When obstacles
out of my hands
allowing them
to lead me astray
taking my eyes off
what He said

Moving with divine flow
letting Him lead
my hands He's been holding

Did I let go?
Do I trust that
He has everything
under control?
Do I allow Him to show Himself?

He says
'never will I leave
nor forsake'
And what does it really mean?

He'll never
lead me astray
completing the
works He started

Never will He leave
nor forsake

He designed my steps
and He's there
every step of the way
every step of everyday

Open divine eyes
to recognize
how He's been there
time after time
all along

in your heart
singing a new song
nothing that comes against you
can get in the way
because He's made sure
it's not more than
you can take
trusting Him to be
everything you need
in the time of need
even when you're feeling unworthy
or you feel you're lacking
He being all sufficiency
a peace transcending understanding
trusting in His name
and that He is your security
He is the comfort
never will He forsake you
never will He leave

20

A Purposeful Life

You're examining your life
Struggling to live in the moment
When the future may not always seem so bright
In your own eyes
God may show you an outcome
Or you may envision yourself in different dreams
And all you're seeing are impossibilities
Wondering if you're the right individual
If God is looking at the right life
He gives you a snippet of an answer
It may bring some clarity
And be a bit more reassuring
And yet you still see impossibilities
Wondering how you can make reality
What you're seeing
Wondering if you're even qualified
Or if it's too late
Asking if you missed the mark
Did you miss the opportunity?
Did you make too many mistakes?
To just be all that you were born to be
Just living by and by
Wondering if there is more to life
If there is more to your life
In your own soul searching,
For the answers
Why I am who I am?
Why did I have to go through..?
Why was I born?
Why am I still here?
After all that
And you're still here
Healthy, breathing
So there is still hope
There is still time
God has you here for a reason
There will be different seasons

And in your life, there is significance
And it's greater than your existence
He can work through you
For you to make a difference
There's more to life than what we can see
What we see in our own lives
May not be God's reality
He has higher ways in His thinking
When beginning with Him, to develop intimacy
He will bring it to memory
That in your whole lifetime
He has never left you hangin'
That's how good He is
And you have yet to see, how good He really is
God's reality
More to life than just you and me
You're not the only one feeling the way you do
Doesn't matter who you are
No matter what you're going through
Doesn't matter what you've done
There is nothing new under the sun
What He says has already been done
There were thoughts of you
Before this world could conceive
When you try to find your place in society
Your true validation will only come from
Getting to know the Creator personally
Being hearkened to the still voice internally
Putting an end to the whys
Why me?
Why am I so important?
Why now?
Why not later?
Why not sooner?
The miraculous of your testimony
God has kept you
And through everything
You are still being
You are okay

God loves you anyway
And He can use someone like you
To let His love, light, and Glory shine
For someone else in need
Purpose is not defined just within our own selves
We must be continually God seeking
For people reaching
Who souls are searching
Trying to find a more meaningful living
Trying to define a purposeful life

A HIGHER CAUSE

You don't see,
how God's constantly working
when facing life's reality.

This journey seems contradictory,
when going against the teaching,
to trust what you sense and see
instead of depending,
upon a Higher Being.

You're experiencing Him everyday,
but you can't explain,
through your own sensory.

Beyond your own ingenuity,
through Him, what you're possessing,
and you're still learning.

It doesn't seem fair!
Not fully understanding
where your life is going.
When you really come to know,
how little you have control.

Doesn't matter,
who you think you are,
or where you might be
nothing in life is guaranteed.

As life happens,
how do you know,
what and who you stand for?

What is your motivation?
Where is your foundation?
What is your Higher Calling?
What is your soul in reach for?
What you never experienced before.

An inner void,
a child that cries within
and you can't explain.

Can't resolve with external things.
What does it all really mean?
How did it all become so confusing?

When relying on what you think you know,
based on what you've seen before.
You might have to take another direction,
Or gain a different life perspective,
Through a Divine perception.

Spiritually sound,
even when it's unheard of.
Logically, life remains a mystery,
on God's word, meditating,
you'll find it's repeated history.

More than what you can imagine:
In His eyes,
You and your life,
have so much more meaning.

More than what you're realizing:
In Him,
Your life is very influential.
Whatever it is you're deciding,
many lives it is affecting.

So in life, you have to be,
willing to go beyond your own satisfactory.
Living for a Higher Cause!
It will be a higher cost.

Fully enacting
what you were born and called to be.
Representing Him,
by standing for humanity!

He Loves Me

He loves me with no capacity
He had to break it down in His divinity,
That I might see the light
And it's been a long time,
Since we've been face to face,
To kiss your lips
And to be guided by,
only the light in your eyes
In the midst of everything,
You were there for me,
When I was blinded and lost in my own darkness,
Your back never faced me
You see, He created me
Before I knew the intimacy, He already had with me
He had been waiting for me, His bride
And all this time, I couldn't conceive
Soul searching, purpose life filled, but lacking
Something was missing
In the time of earthly searching
My spirit thirsty, soul weary,
But in what well doing?
He gave me life eternity,
because He loves me
I did what I didn't intend
Never the less, He gave me rest,
Restoration
He said, "New Beginning"
And still makes His presence known daily
He feeds me His peace, His laughter
He comforts me, He forgave me
He makes it easy to do all the right things,
Because I love Him as He loves me
And I am tasting His goodness;
I clothe Him as I sing His praises
He's done so much for me
He was there all along
Cupping my every tears,

Quieting my worries and fears
He outweighed my heavy heart
Renewing my mind,
Refreshing my breath
My heart carries another tune
As I stand in confidence in Him,
In knowing He's got me covered
I belong to Him,
His words reside within me
He shows me in everything,
love is the key
Questing around the corner,
and the answer is Him
In Him I lack nothing,
For forever more He reigns
I'm apart of the bloodline,
Of His royal family.
He passes His torch of love to share,
Just because He cares
You see it's the little things He does
To show how much He loves
In spite of me being me He does
In lonely or company He still loves
Great is His grace and mercies
And I am filled with serenity
Sustaining life's adversities
Freeing me from captivity
And in Him I find completeness
Granted life more abundantly
As I see His hearts display,
On Calvary
All because He loves me.

Foundational Prayer

Lord help me to walk more with confidence in who I am in you, freely being the best me I can be, that you may show yourself. Help me not to weigh myself down with people's false expectations of me. Help me to have faith that I am worthy enough for your cause. Thank you for giving me a sense of purpose. To daily be more centered in your will. Thank you for being faithful enough to complete the works you began in me. For this I am ever so grateful. In Christ name, so be it.

CHAPTER TWO:

Trusting the Process

Personal Reflection: Trusting the Process

No matter what I face in life, there is a process, and that didn't change when I became born-again. For me acknowledging Christ in my life was more of acknowledging that I can't make it on my own, not without Him. God loves all of us, and gave us all a free will. I learned that if I want Him to really intervene in my life, I have to come to Him willingly and whole-heartedly and believe in who He says He is.[10]

Although I could learn from somebody else's faith, I could not depend upon it. I had to learn for myself, who and how real God is, and that nothing will separate me from His love and his promises. It's a truth that's not easily accepted or received in the midst of going through different circumstances and transitions. Or when I am having a hard time with being consistent and making the right type of decisions for myself.

It has taken some time for me to learn to trust the process. I used to be very independent and self-sufficient. I had a lot of pride and wouldn't allow myself to rely on anybody. I had to be in control of everything, I had to do everything and fret if things wouldn't go just the way I planned.[11] After allowing God to intervene in my life things has changed. The trusting process has been very humbling for me, because I went from being self-sufficient to being God-sufficient. Trusting Him like I never trusted[12] Him before. Allowing Him to work out, and work through others to assist me along the way to where He's taking me.

I know it was easier for me to focus on my problems and to worry about what was going on around me. I allowed myself to be distracted, being so easily moved by whatever was thrown at me. I would be at the verge of giving up due to feelings of inadequacy, insignificance, or doubt. My emotions were my dictator, and because of that I was very unstable. In those times, I've learned that I'm usually close to a breakthrough, I just need to keep persevering.[13] To look at my life from God's perspective and not my own, through His Word. Staying focused on the bigger picture.[14]

Trusting the process is trusting God. It entails allowing God to handle what I am not able to on my own. That's what it's about, walking by faith and not by sight.[15] This is a process in itself since society teaches us to only trust the seen, and not the unseen.[16] I have learned to have faith that God has already taken care of and provided for all my needs-even at those moments when I'm trying to make ends meet!

The process of trusting has taught me the importance of endurance. Not giving up or in to trials or temptations I face and walking in confidence in who God is. I can't rely[17] on what I think I know, or what others think. All I have to do is trust and have faith. Faith is the confident assurance that what we hope for is going to happen. It is the evidence of things we cannot see.[18] I have to believe in who He says[19] I am and who He is, what He says I will have and what He can do. Even though, I may not know how, when and why, I have to allow Him to have His way, in keeping in mind that it's all working together.

Trusting the process, that He has my best interest at heart and the different phases in life I enter into are building character, and equipping me for a brighter future.[20] Trusting the process, and trusting that nothing is too hard or [21]impossible for God and that nothing will separate me from His love.[22] Trusting the process, allowing Him the different opportunities to show Himself to be even bigger than what I imagined Him to be.[23] Trusting the process, trusting Him through the journey that it will be promising and fulfilling for His purpose.

The Process of a Purposeful Life

It's so easy sometimes to get
Wrapped up in your own world
Feeling sorry for yourself
Like nobody cares
Feeling like you're on the verge of losing it
When you've actually won it
And flying ever so freely
You've yet to realize that
You already have the victory
You have already won the race
Things have already worked themselves out
Through your acknowledgement of
God's infallible love
But even in knowing that
You still feel the need to sweat those minute things
Instead of focusing on the joy someone brings
What you are facing
Is a reflection of what's going on inside
This warfare,
Battle of the mind
You carry the ball
So you determine how this game is going to go
Being conscious of what
You're aiming the ball towards
You make the choice
Taking responsibility of handling life's difficulties
And in those times of adversity
The real time, when you really need to shine
That's how God wants to show Himself
Through you and your life of Divine prime
Your testimony: where you've been,
Where you are, where you're headed
Lessen the need to self rely
Recognizing God's strength on inside
You can't be discouraged or dismayed about the process
Process of learning and growing
Process of loving and ascending

Sometimes stumbling and falling
Process of the image of God being
To find worth and value in yourself and life
You have to learn to see through God's eyes
Which comes in time with seeking His face
Because that's the only thing in this world
That will never change
Accepting God's strategy of defining life successfully
Making life more fulfilling
By living it more collectively
Finding more meaning
Building bridges to be constantly connecting
It may fill that sense of belonging
Finding creativity for the stars to be reaching
It's easy to feel self-pity
It's easy to experience complacency
Won't get you near your destiny
How you position yourself in times of uncertainty
And how much of God are you really seeking
Will be determinant of a lot of things
How much of you, will you sacrifice
Willingly to come outside of yourself
And recognize
That you've been taken care of
What you're facing has already been handled
How do you let your Glory light shine
And allow His love to manifest through and for you
When you're searching for answers
And trying to figure out
How it's all coming together
When you're faced with something that feels like eternity
In reality
It's just for a season
You're only facing what God knows you can face
Each day even unrecognized
He still manifests His love, mercy and grace
In seeking His face
And trying to feel His warm embrace
Know that your steps are ordered
And you are in the right place.

In the Meantime

as I learn to trust and walk your ways
I discover my own limitations
and find that I make many mistakes
but you knew already
somehow
it is still to your Glory
according to your purpose
part of your plan
but when I mess up,
I worry
scared to miss
my purpose, your calling
scared of mishandling
what's in stored for me
yes, I am your child
you are greater than
whatever I could aspire
yet I'm still a human being
I falter and fall time after time
you just dust me off
and say, "keep going"
when I received salvation
you forgave all my transgressions
and I still say,
"yes to your will and ways"
it feels like
I'm going the wrong way,
some days
but you say everything is in place
and it makes perfect sense
I can't explain to myself or anybody else
right now, with you
what I've just experienced
sometimes,
that has been discouraging
time after time
learning to take things,

one day at a time
I'll just happen to
in your time,
stumble into the right time and place
where Destiny awaits
but in the meantime
not taken for granted and trusting
right now, where you have me
making the most of everything
learning to recognize right now,
how you're working
making me more pliable
molding me
that you may use me
to the fullest potentiality
I don't want to be
full of what you could have used
full of what the world needs
and be in the grave asleep
and in the meantime
it's a lot of sacrifices
a daily process
to embrace a new day
a new way
but do Lord,
what is necessary
to get me ready
to live more in love,
effectively
and in the meantime
continue to be the Way
I anticipate the different ways,
you'll show your face
lead the way
reassure me of
your strength, your presence
and everything will be as you say

Things aren't always what they seem

Sometimes, you find that you want to just give in.
When you try to follow the right path,
Things appear to be so enticing.

And you don't want to stand alone
in what you're feeling.
Because in reality,
You could be doing a lot of things.

This constant warfare
Who is to win?
The battle of the spirit vs. the lust of the sin

Through the end,
God is telling you that He's got you
He is telling you that, He's with you

Even when it doesn't seem...
Yet He's teaching you faith...
To reach for, speak on
What His word reveals and conveys

The trick to seeing is being able to see
When you are standing,
And truly waiting on God.
Allowing Him to be in all control.

It's a process,
But when it's all Him, it's the best.
Because He has your best interest.

Sometimes you want to give in
To temptation
Reaching for short-lived pleasures

You're itching to receive
That which takes timing
To make sure
You're really ready

Your anxiety
Could drive you
To settle for less or all wrongness
Because the best is not easily apprehended

You try to endure, nevertheless
And always what's good for you,
Has to be worked a little harder for.
It will cost you a bit more.

Walking in His goodness,
Defines discipline.
Is what place God wants you in,

Because He loves you.
In Him your soul will find rest.
Filled with peace that surpasses all understanding.

He deserves your life, your love and your all.
Because no one can do for you,
Like He does.
Because He cares so much about you.

There is the road of uncertainty.
A road crossed by many beings.
Because it's not always comfortable,
Or what makes sense.

It's just the right thing to do:
To wait, to trust,
And to have faith.
Things aren't always what they seem.

Leaning to Own Understanding

Lord, I don't know
What's the next step after believing?
Knowing and receiving that I have a calling
Constantly met with frustration.
Trying to seek out consolation
Only left with confusion
In what I believe you're telling me
Sometimes it feels contradictory
In getting to know you,
answers I'm still searching
Grant me a peace of mind
Sometimes in the midst of a crowd
I stand on my own, all alone
You said, you'll never leave nor forsake me
Nobody feeling the words you're saying to me
But I know it's not about them or me
You say you're All-seeing, All-knowing
My life is on the line!
And all you're saying is, "Trust me"
I put you before me
Trying to follow your righteous lead
Left with what feels like chaos, commotion
You're a God of order
And nothing seems in place
I'm losing my mind trying to find
How things are coming together
And I don't want to go back to what I was doing
But when I receive your peace
And remain still in my own capacity and space
I only want to be brought back to
Your thoughts of me when forming
You never said it was going to be easy
In your presence is where I want to be
I've got to believe
There's a season
And at times I will be tested
I have to walk in what you say I am

Walk in what you say I have
Walk in what you say I can do
I've got to believe in who I am in You
And who You are to me
Believing requires accountability
Direct me where I need to be
And when life happens
Help me to remain in that firmly
Please comfort me in those times of weary
Your words are the most reassuring
Grant me a peace about trusting you,
If not a full understanding
In you my trust shall remain
And you say in faith I will see...
I just realized, that I asked you,
To increase my faith and trust in you
And you've just given me the opportunity to...

Put Your Trust In Me

Put your trust in Me.
Have faith in Me and you'll see.
Learn of Me.
Understand that I am He.
Look inside your heart with sincere honesty,
Will you not perceive that I've done a new thing?
Put your trust in Me.
And I will not depart from:
My words, My decrees, My promises,
To you from Me
Oh My promises,
Are yea and amen.
My child, do you not see?
See that I have your best interest.
I have ordered your steps in your calling.
I can sense the urgency of the flesh,
But if you could fully see what I see,
You wouldn't be ready.
I am God.
A God who is bigger than your education.
A God who is bigger than your imagination.
Bigger than your sense of direction.
Bigger than any of your situations.
Bigger than your life.
Bigger than your predestined destiny.
Bigger than your blessings.
A God who is bigger than your calling.
Bigger than any life's lessons.
Trust Me, invest in Me.
Have faith, and you'll see.
My words are reassuring.
I have loved you, I have honored you.
I am with you with everything you say or do.
I cherish you.
I think about and trouble Myself over you.
Because I have called you,
For My own Glory.

So, for your life, will, and ways:
Allow Me the honor,
Of handling your daily cares and concerns.
Allow Me the honor of blessing you.
Allowing Me the honor of receiving your praises.
Come and meet Me face to face.
Let Me be the one to fulfill those desires.
Let Me be the answer.
Let Me be your strength.
Let Me be your security.
Let Me fight your battles.
You be the warrior, I'll take your worries.
Be patient, I'm patient, it's a process.
Constant dying of the flesh.
Don't stress what you can't handle by yourself.
That is what I'm here for.
Don't confuse yourself trying to figure out,
What you feel is chaos.
Everything makes perfect sense to Me.
Have faith and you'll see.
Put your trust in Me.

Trusting Prayer

Lord, with all that is going on, help me to continue to acknowledge you in everything. Help me to trust your will and your ways. Trusting you with an understanding that whatever it is you ask of me, that you know what is best. Help me not to worry about things out of my control. Help me to recognize more how you're working and to trust the process, being confident that it's all going to work together for the good. For this I am grateful. In Christ name I pray, Amen.

CHAPTER THREE:

Experiencing God

Personal Reflection: Experiencing God

In a book called *Experiencing God*, Henry T. Blackaby and Claude V. King talk about how an individual's way of viewing things changes when his/her life is in the midst of where God is. I have always been told growing up how 'God works in mysterious ways.' In time I raised the question inside: if God's ways are so mysterious, can I afford to limit who He is and what He is capable of doing in and through my life? For me, at a very young age God had shown me that He had me here for a reason, and for a long time that was my motivation in life, having a sense of purpose. Being brought up in the church, it was so easy to conform to tradition and religious practice, relying on certain activities and not really coming to know Him personally. I could throw up confetti prayers and sing praise and worship songs to Him at church and still not reach God. For me it was easier to try to do what everybody else was doing, than to have my own personal experience with God. If nothing else, I at least looked like I knew what I was doing.

Temporarily I forfeited knowing how God wants to deal with and reach me in His own unique way that He knows will get my attention. It's so easy to get caught up in an image and the outside appearance instead coming from the heart, being real and transparent. In focusing more on accomplishing these things, I was more self-centered instead of being God-centered. Upon saying yes to Christ, it's a constant process of thinking less of myself and more of what God wants. I started to understand what it means when it says in the Bible that God looks at the heart, while as human beings we tend to look at the outward appearances.[24]

I did have to learn that God does want me to be prosperous and to experience living abundantly in this lifetime. He sometimes grants me my desires, just to show me that He knows my heart.[25] He wants me to have full confidence[26] as His child to receive His promises[27] and His blessings.[28] Also to experience His full glory[29] and richness by living up to who He says[30] I am, what He says I have and what I will do, according to my faith.[31] Yet, it still cannot replace having a personal relationship with Him. That's why for me, I have to learn to continually keep everything that is being done to, for and through me in the right perspective, His perspective.

God was not impressed by my lengthy prayers, how well I sang to Him, or how many church activities I was involved in. He was more concerned with my coming from the heart, really coming to know Him, and demonstrating love, compassion, and forgiveness for others. He was dealing with me about putting my heart where my mouth was, at those times that I want to acknowledge or talk to Him. I can't reflect who He is if I'm not sincerely striving to come to know Him and experience Him daily.

In my own experience, I learned that God is always ahead of me in time. That means the things He asks of me, even though I may be equipped, I have to rely on Him to bring to pass what He says as if it is the reality of that time. So when He wants to take me to another level, I can't stay where I am to get to where He is. For me writing this book was definitely a faith thing, and I had to definitely make some major adjustments in my life. I've always been very conscious of what I say because I know the power of words. It was important to me to 'spoon my own medicine' and to make sure I was practicing what I preach. Writing this book in faith, I knew I was going to be accountable to the things I said, so I had to do some growing up in areas, and continually deny myself, and constantly seek God so that the book will accomplish what He intended.

Doing a book at this time in my life was not in my plan, but it was in God's. In writing this book, I have been going through many different transitions. The book became my own therapy and it ministered to me first. This is important, so that it can come from the heart, where God wants to operate. I know that God really wants to reveal who He is daily to me, in ways not limited to my own abilities, or the normal ritual and religious practice. That has been part of my way of experiencing Him and His realness. Even in His Word, He revealed Himself and worked in many different unorthodox ways through miracles and revelations that He may be glorified.

I know for me it was and still is very important to connect with and seek[32] God, to talk to Him whole-heartedly.[33] For in my experience, I've come to know Him as not just the Creator, but the source and strength of my life. It takes persistence, patience, and a sensitive, open and honest heart to hear and experience a still voice or presence of peace and clarity of the truth.[34] I have to continually choose to remain in God, in His word that I may understand more what He's asking me. In doing this I've gained more discernment and understanding of where and how God is working in my life. He works through the hearts of people, and it can determine how well I connect with the ones I face throughout the day.

It's something to learn to trust[35] that He knows and is the Way. That He knows and will provide the best, and that I'll experience Him as the light and life of every situation[36] that I may encounter. Now I really understand the importance of having a personal relationship with God and how nothing else will compensate for that. It makes life much more fulfilling and meaningful as I reverence Him. As I continue to come to know Him by experience I am able to put more confidence in who He is and what He is capable of doing in and through my life.

Experiencing God

Striving to be
More involved in God's presence
Seeking His will
Through the many life lessons
And then trying to fulfill
It's a step that
Can't be taken lightly
A step no where near easy
At times demanding more reaching
Internally
Pressing, sometimes causing heavy breathing
Experiencing frustration
Dying to views of normality
What you're use to seeing
Increase of expectancy
When you're
Aiming more for the impossibilities
Is how big God wants to be
It's a way of living
You have to choose
God showing Himself through you
In the process of going through
Still have to run through
You still have to go through
The FIRE
But it will not set you ablaze
Because of His amazing Grace
In spite of, you choose to
Continue to run the race
Move forward
Reach towards and upwards
Go beyond your own comfort and capabilities
Just watch and see
What He can do through you
For you
Continue to sit at His feet

To experience Him intimately
Trusting His wisdom and judgment
Upon receiving guidance and clarity
In the direction you're moving
Remaining humble before His Majesty
It'll take place in His time, elevating
It's a...
Day by day Battle
Day by day Choice
In walking out His will for your life
Day by day Peace
Day by day Love and Grace

Experiencing God in your own special way
It may be illogical
Unorthodox
Causing more suffering
To change a way of thinking or believing
Changing a way of living
You have to keep going

Have to keep growing
Accepting limitations of what you control
Can't overrule what He says is so
Believing that He is trustworthy

Believing Him in life,
That you're deserving
Through Him experiencing
And you just accepting.

To Him the Glory

Help Me!
To get my heart ready,
That I might receive,
What you have in store for me.
Reign your Majesty!
I can't continue on worrying,
About something that is your doing.
I just want to be in your will Lord.
Day by day,
I want to get more out of the way.
Because the works I'm doing,
Is not even working.
Hasn't even caught your attention.
I said "yes" to your will.
Increased my commitment for you.
Not realizing the price I would have to pay,
In experiencing you in my own way.
Quickly deceived,
When only expecting Grace and Glory.
Not even considering,
The process of purifying.
In the FIRE!
The FIRE!
I can feel the HEAT!
And you show me you're there.
And I can still feel the HEAT!
Constantly dying to the ways I know.
Showing me areas of my heart,
That you're displeased.
And it hurts me so!
Fooling myself in believing,
That I had it all together.
Being deceived,
When I thought I had the answers.
In Him I'm more depending.
And that's how He wants it to be.
All about Him, and not about me.
To Him all the Glory!

Consecration

Consecration
Standing, sitting still
Inside spiritually reaching
Wondering
Direction seeking
Constantly praying
Remaining in silence
Waiting for the truth
Alleviate the pain
Of going through
Longsuffering
Mouth is closed
Soul is fed
Where the spirit man is led
Through the still voice
Voice of truth
Voice of love and reason
Clear awakening
The dawn of day
Where the yoke breaks
Where the eyes inside, can see
Watching faith
What has been already
Given guidance and clarity
Inner core connecting
Foundational finding
Inner man leads
Faithfully winning
Through consecration, intercession
You freeze
To your time
To your surroundings
Quietly seeking
To have divine encountering
Checking in on timing
Of everything
Attuned to hearkening

Experiencing serenity
To change your attitude
Instead of the situation
You view
Take time with Him
To make most of times
To lessen the stress
To arise
To be the light
Focus
Walking in assurance
In clarity
Allowing Him to shine
Through you, for everybody
Humbling when learning
To live more for Him
To please
Day by day
Not taken for granted
Or missing opportunities
With inner ears listening
Tender heart ready
To be wherever God is working
To hear what He's saying
To daily practice loving
Through consecrating
Coming to spiritual understanding
Interceding
When thinking of Him
For others
Constantly thank Him
Taking a prayer breath
To constantly breathe life
To bring life
Love, hope and peace
With inner ears listening
Tender heart ready
To be wherever He's working
Hearing what He's saying
To daily practice loving

REMAIN IN ME

Can you undo what I've already done
Can your own will outweigh Mine
You are in search for answers
That can't be defined,
By what you see in your eyes
Look inside and see
And as you remain in Me
You possess the key
To what you're looking for
Remember to remain in Me
Yes, experience My strength and might
Be pliable, be free
Be mobile
Allowing Me,
To work through you and your life freely
Oh, taste and see
Be encouraged, be confident
In all that you stand for
From you,
I will not withhold any good thing
This is a new thing, I'm doing
A new day, you're experiencing
Now living life more abundantly
Living more freely
Not living up to any expectations,
Outside of Me
I had access to you
Before this world could even imagine you
How can they process your full capability
Your full potentiality
Without understanding who you are in Me
Who you are to Me
Your life is in no better hands
Your heart can not be better treated
Your destiny to Me has so much clarity
Remain in Me
Because I am, in you

Bearing much fruit
Pursue Me, chose Me
Try Me, and see what I can do
Your labor is not in vain
I can see your heart
And what is going on
Remember, I see everything
Beforehand, I saw it coming
And I have been preparing you
I called you in such a time as this
Remain steadfast in Me,
And you'll see
Get ready
For what is upcoming
Get ready, get ready, get ready
When all things work together
It keeps getting better and better
Keep moving, keep seeking Me dilligently
Wait and see
What you're entitled to
Have no fear
No man can take from you
I will not withhold from you
And that is My word
Stay encouraged
Let Me be your direction,
For I am the way, the truth and the life
With Me there's so much entity
And you are still learning of your inheritance
Your entitlements
It's alright
Move with the light
I'm with you all the time
More than what you realize
When you really come to understand
No one can take from Me,
For you, what I hold in My hand
And oh, how much I love you

Is it meant to be meant for me?

Whatever it is
that you're wondering
if it is meant to be
will be your determining

Pondering on the meaning
of the abundant life
and when does it begin

Could it be
that God wants you
to have in life
the finer things

He wants for you to have
His very best
but it's your call
if you chose to settle for less
instead of trusting and waiting on Him

When it comes to your desires
you're use to things that easily expire
going beyond measures to have
to keep
finding what works for you
is a task

It's not easy
understanding in His eyes
that you're worthy
and how much you're worth
just for being His child

But how do you grasp that concept
when you never really encountered
nor really aspired
to posses beyond your own standards

Because you're use to not taking
accepting or receiving
So you miss out
and you allow someone else
to be left out on the blessings

Not requiring anything out of the ordinary
scared to reach for the extraordinary
not even phased with material things

But outside of that
there are so many things
you've yearned for
that you've done without

You've missed opportunities
you don't even ask for anything
in His name

Not even decreeing or claiming
because the desires you do have
you feel aren't tangible
so you rather lack

You're feeling your own longing
is too silly
and to ask for from God
is too complicated

And He's saying
you lack because
you don't ask
Because when you believe
what you ask
you will receive

And when you believe
what you'll receive
it'll take some preparing

What it really means to receive
upscaling faith
planting more seeds
of belief
being a blessing
to someone else in need

Upon receiving
you'll handle the maintaining
Understanding His plans
His reasoning
for your prosperity
an abundant ending

Giving you hope
a future and security
in the name of His love
everlasting love

Overriding the fear
the fear of missing out
on the best thing
Fearing something or someone greater
greater than what you can imagine
Fearing that you can't handle it
fear of losing it all

Learning to keep it
all in His perspective
not taking it for granted
by allowing it define
your being, your essence

Keeping Him priority
confiding in Him

to be all that you need
beyond your provider
and security
a friend in the time of need

In walking in the name
of His love,
everlasting love
you have access
to what you dare to dream
the things you deemed
as impossibilities
delighting in Him
He'll bring it all to reality
with Him experiencing

Prayer of Excellence

Heavenly Father, I thank you for the work that you began in me, and for moving it towards its completion. Without you my life has no meaning and I cannot fulfill my destiny. Help me to live my life <u>now</u> more abundantly and to trust you at all times. I thank you for opening my eyes that I may be more aware of how I'm experiencing you on the daily basis. I want to take the time right now to thank you, even before I have all the answers to everything. I thank you for my richness in you. I thank you for the gifts you've given me to bless others. As a good steward, help me to demonstrate your excellence through integrity in my daily encounter with people, my health, my financial and emotional well being. Help me to be more focused, ready and willing to be used as your vessel. Thank you for guidance. Thank you for strength. Thank you for wisdom. Thank you for your greatest gift of all, love. In Jesus name, I pray, Amen.

CHAPTER FOUR:

Two-Steppin' with God

Personal Reflection: Two-Steppin' with God

I remember facing some different transitions towards the end of 2003 and into the beginning of 2004. I was just coming out of a job, and was facing different dilemmas trying to figure out where God was in my situation. I was fretting to God about not liking where I was, and whatever it was He was trying to do. I remember clearly being interrupted by His still voice saying, "dance with me." I was then given this whole vision with the concept of dancing with God.

The scenario was: *I was at some sort of social setting and I peeped somebody at the center of the dance floor that I was feelin', and so I decided to join the person. Once I get to the center, I try to keep up with this person even though they're doing some unusual, unfamiliar things, or the music switches up (and I'm either not feeling the music, or having a hard time keeping up with the change of music with this person). And all I know is that I'm feeling this person like no other, and so I do my best to keep up with him. And I get to the point where I'm so into this person and into what I'm doing with this person that I forget about what is going on around me.*

That's how it is when I make the decision to join God where He's working. God was saying "dance with me; let me lead the dance to your life." Just trust me and lean on me, have faith[37] and you'll see." It's really learning to move with the Spirit and go with the divine flow.

Henry T. Blackaby's and Claude V. King's *Experiencing God* discusses how I can try to be organized as I want to be in life, but obviously things don't always go as I would like. There always tends to be a lot of unexpected happenings. Even in the midst of making plans and setting goals, God just may come without prior notice with His own agenda. He's there with His own strategy of doing things. It's more on how I handle the "interruptions" or "divine interventions" because His ways and thoughts are so much higher than my own.

I'm learning more and more to go with the flow, to be patient and to just two-step with God. Two-steppin' with God is taking it one day at a time [38] and living more in the moment. With faith, being more cooperative and not being concerned with the end results of what's going to happen. Being sensitive enough at heart to keep up with God's moves on the daily basis no matter how big or small the steps might be. I have recognized God as my strength,[39] fortress and refuge, as I depend on, stick with, and allow Him to fight my battles for me. Even in the midst of facing fears, going through different transitions, growing phases;[40] when I am out of my comfort zone, and facing my worst-could-happen situations or I'm entering into strange [41] places that appear to be dark, where I have to rely on God's Word[42] to see me through.

For me dancing is very relaxing and enjoyable, it helps me to take my mind off a lot of things. I had to learn that God doesn't want me to worry about a thing and to leave whatever is out my hands in His. He didn't intend for me to have a distressful life,[43] but a healthy one. He does want me to take care of what He has given me, which includes my body, my mind, spirit, the gifts He placed inside of me as well as His tangible blessings that surround me.

Dancing is a very intimate thing, and to really two-step with Him, takes a level of intimacy, trust, and understanding that one is really resting in Him. Where His presence is, there is fullness of joy,[44] peace, [45]and love. I know for me, I'm at the point of only trying to be part of wherever He is. Without limiting where He might be in a particular time. That's why His ways are so mysterious, that I can't just place Him in a box. Sometimes where He is, it's a blessing in disguise. I can predict, that He will guide me, but I just can't predict how. At times it gets worse before it gets better, but I know if I hang in there long enough and do my best to keep up with Him, my focus usually changes, the situation itself may not change right away, but how I view it or where my[46] attention is tends to change. I don't always like the music, but I'm trying to keep up with my dance partner. God has shown me that He has His own rhythm in my life and that He was just waiting for me to follow Him.

Dancing with Him, resting[47] and remaining in Him. Staying focused, encouraged and confident.[48] I can be more honest about where I am, and who I am. Daily I choose to stay attuned to where He leads, so that I may follow. It's not always easy, and at times it takes some adjustments. I have learned that it's so much better, healthier for me to go with the spiritual flow, and not to always try to take the initiative of making things happen, (especially in a certain way).

I do believe whatever God intended for me, I will have, and that He will withhold no good thing from me. There is no reason for me to be anxious, besides the fact that when things are forced it's usually not natural or the real thing. God is real, His love is the real thing, and it's nothing forceful about it, that's just His nature.[49] Two-Steppin' with God, is all about learning to trust God, understanding worth[50] in God, accepting His peace[51] and experiencing His love and through it all, really coming to know Him as The Way, The Truth and The Life.[52]

Even though: Psalms 23:4

Even though I walk in life through valleys as dark as death. A state of stagnation and dry hopes like weeds that are standing in areas where my dreams lie beneath, that I feel should be flourishing. Walking through the valley dark and not lovely; where the only light I see is God's Word a lamp unto my feet. Sometimes that's the only light I can receive in the midst of contemplating how life's worth living. When I am facing my worst-could-happens situations. And I recognize how I'm truly being tested. To see if I will join God, where He's already rested. Waiting for me to get to the point of surrendering, serenity attuned to hearing and willing to follow His lead. Walking through the valleys facing mirages of what's tantalizing, enticing, but temporary. Taken off track to where I'm actually headed (even though it doesn't look like it). And He's saying, "trust me". So I can recognize His strength in me. I can see that this stop is temporary. Doesn't determine my becoming. Even though I can't always see through the valleys where He's taking me. Even when it resembles what I don't want to face, because I feel I won't make it. I feel I won't survive, fighting to stay alive. To keep the dream alive. Yes, even in those times. Storms come to sift the life out of me. But I cannot be moved. I will not be moved. Even though I walk through those valleys that appear to be life threatening. Even though I rome through areas in life that are destructive. I shall have no fear. I shall not be moved. For His love, His protection overshadows me, encompasses me. Keeping me, even when I didn't feel kept. My strength and fortress. Keeping me in a safe place. A haven. A sacred place. At the end of the rope, through adversity, He's still with me. Even though I walk through the valley, not knowing where He's taking me, or what is coming my way. I will not sway like the wind. I shall have no fear, and I will rest in His secret place, because I know who lives inside of me.

Resting Tempo

meditation
relax, breathe
now count to three
one, two, three
now take a deep breath
inhale
now, exhale
be free
free
don't forget to shut
your windows of your
mind
and keep your mouth
closed
but listen for serenity
listen for love
listen for the truth
joy in dwelling
shh
forget about
 what's going on around you
live for today
live for this moment
quiet, quiet, quiet
right there
right there
relax
be at ease
let the tension
be relieved
it's okay
at where you are
know who and whose you are
listen for your
resting tempo
shhh

I don't have the answers
you don't either
live, breathe, hope
let it go
and let God
surrender
let go of that monster
let Him take that from you
it's not good for you
release
don't intake
so much you allow
to consume you
it was not intended
all you have to do
live, breathe, hope
just be
just be
just breathe
now count to three
one, two, three
let go
live
breathe
be
believe
be free
relax
receive the peace
receive the peace
receive the peace

A peace that covers
what you can't explain
keeping you from
acting out emotionally
hard times facing
all of life's demands
to leave it all in
the Master's hands
though it's hard to comprehend
facing challenges
trying to figure out solutions
losing focus
when taking eyes off
enduring prize
tis the season
take the peace
continue to plant the seeds
you will soon reap
this is faith acting
your temp rising
instead of being at ease
taking a deep breath
enjoy living
He'll provide what you need
He didn't intend
for you to be stressing
back aching
heart racing
hair losing
eye twitching
in fear and agony
trying to control everything
walking unlovingly
sleeping insecurely
self-neglecting
appetite changing
fear of losing

full of pride
feeling self-justified
instead of loving God enough
to direct your life
self-discredit
not loving enough
to grow, make mistakes
to edit
forgiveness
all already covered
on His love credit
take the peace
breathe
then listen to
what He's saying
to you
through your life
no matter the strife
walking in love
and being guided by the light
with faith
putting on a good fight
not with fist and might
focus on
the enduring prize
God has called you to
good health
not just abundant life
righteous wealth
taking care of self
mind, body, as well as spiritually
attitude determining everything
daily you're choosing
to take the peace
instead of worrying
leaving with God
what you're not handling
to take care of all of your needs
learn to appreciate

and to be more forgiving
not forgetting that you,
are a work in progress
being more honest and at ease
take the peace
and humble yourself
before His Majesty
allow Him to
help you to
be all you can be
without the
risk of
stressing
and missing out
and really enjoy living
remember to stick with Him
to stay at ease
no matter what is happening
you can do all things
and by His strength
and love shed
receive the peace

Living A Victorious Life

There's no need
for me
to be anxious
or grow weary
in well doing
because
what God says
is for me
will be
will be
and from me
He will withhold
no good thing

There's no need
for me to stress
to make happen
what He says
will be reality
it will happen
in His timing
that He may
get the Glory

Whether
He chooses
to work through me
or whatever
He chooses
to do for me
waiting to show
His reality
because it's not about me
just ways for
you and I
to recognize
His identities

Throughout lifetime
time after time

no age, color, gender,
circumstance or status defined
just God choosing
what this world denies
and God using
His prime
the ones He knows
the Divine will shine

In everyday
transparencies
His light will shine
through realities
miraculous mysteries
of love actualities
because that's His nationality

As you see
for me to be
the child of the Most High
I got to get you
to recognize
the abundant life
in this lifetime
I pray
God will use me
to continue to choose me
to work through me
that you won't
see me,
but see,
He

I'm not trying
to be focused
on the materialistic
what's tangible to me
because if that's where
my focus is limited
then it might as well

be the end for me
got to keep
eyes on eternity

I want people
to see He
God in me
working through me
blessing me
helping me to "no stress"
through adversity
demonstrating
love and peace

Not growing anxious
or weary
in well doing
because what God says
will be reality
not just for here and now
but for eternity
it will be
kingdom building

Coming to see
like God sees
definitely an awakening
in this lifetime
no time for playing
striving is limited
if this or here
is just the focus
it's where you choose
to spend
eternity
choosing
abundant living
beginning of everlasting
where God wants us to be

I'm striving more and more
to live stress free
living honestly

living of life
full of love and peace
no matter what
surrounds me
allowing God
to show Himself
through me

A life of peace
founded in love
rooted in God
walking in love
to walk with God
and that's all
there is to it
to reflect
His image
knowing
Him personally
allowing Him to
use you
as a light for
humanity

No matter where
your territory
walking in authority
there's no room for fear
no room for
the enemy to defeat
only room for victory
no ending to
abundant living
in God
the founder
the Way, the Truth
and the Life
helping others see
 the light
by demonstrating
living a victorious life.

TWO-STEPPIN' WITH GOD

As I step into this place
As though I can see your face
Even though I can't
You are
still more real to me
Than in life,
what I'm facing
As I continue to experience you personally
I can see how I'm following your lead
Leading me by the waters of peace
Helping me to remain still, calm
Like a newborn spring breeze
I can be on the scene
In how you renewed life within me
Especially you loved me
You wrapped your arms around me
Held and kept me
Watching over me
We are looking at my reflection
And you are seeing something different
from what I see
And you love what you see
More than what I can imagine being
Of a image of God being
And as I remain on the scene,
I see
Faithful to the works
you began in me
And in you, I'm made
fearfully and wonderfully
Breath of life
Each day, more and more
My heart becomes more
in sync to your tune
And as we dance
I can flow with your flow
I don't always like the music playing

But as I dance with you
And I can make room
To learn your groove
When you play a new tune
And my heart will go "ba boom"
Like the branches to the vine
I will remain in you
And you shall in me
And we will bear good fruit
As much as I am into you
And begin to feel your groove
No good could I produce
If I ever be without you
When the waters are troubled
And I'm down in the weary
Music's playing dreary
Wondering how things could be
You perform your strength and might
Lord,
For me, what you've done
To me, as you are
For others help me to
Love and be the light.

Guidance prayer

Heavenly Father I just thank you for caring about the direction my life is going. I ask that you will continue to give me guidance. Thank you for ordering my steps. Help me to be more willing to go with the flow, especially when things aren't going as I would like. Help me to continue to acknowledge you in everything I do, and to see more of how you are constantly working on my behalf. I thank you that in you I don't want or have to be anxious for anything. On a daily basis, help me more to demonstrate the abundant and victorious life in you. I thank you for your gifts of love and everlasting life. Thank you for showing yourself to be the way, the truth and the life. I praise you and give you all the glory, in Jesus name, Amen.

Scripture Notes

Chapter One: He Loves Me
Page 15

1 I John 4:9,19 NLT "God showed how much he loved us by sending his only Son into the world so that we might have eternal life through him." "We love each other* 1 as a result of his loving us first."

2 I John 4:12 NLT "No one has ever seen God. But if we love each other, God lives in us, and his love has been brought to full expression through us."

3 Psalms139:14 NLT "Thank you for making me so wonderfully complex! Your workmanship is marvelous—and how well I know it."

4 Romans 8:28 NLT "And we know that God causes everything to work together* 2 for the good of those who love God who and are called according to his purpose for them."

5 I John 4:16 NLT "We know how much God loves us, and we have put our trust in him. God is love, and all who live in love live in God, and God lives in them."

   John 15:5 NLT "Yes, I am the vine' you are the branches. Those who remain in me, and I in them, will produce much fruit. For apart from me you can do nothing."

6 Isaiah 43:4 NLT "Others died that you might live. I traded their lives for yours because you are precious to me. You are honored, and I love you."

7 Hebrews 13:5 NLT, "...God has said, 'I will never fail you. I will never forsake you.'"

   Matthew 28:20 NLT "...And be sure of this: I am with you always, even to the end of the age."

Page 16

8 I Thessalonians 3:12 NLT "And may the Lord make your love grow and overflow to each other and to everyone else, just as our love overflows towards you."

9 I John 4:18 NLT "Such love has no fear because perfect love expels all fear..."

Chapter Two: Trusting the Process
Page 31

10 Hebrews 11:6 NLT "So, you see, it is impossible to please God without faith. Anyone who wants to come to him must believe that there is a God and that he rewards those who sincerely seek him."

11 Proverbs 16:9 NLT "We can make our plans, but the LORD determines our steps."

12 Psalms 20:7 NLT "Some nations boast of their armies and weapons,* 3 but we boast in the LORD our God."

13 Hebrews 10:36 NLT "Patient endurance is what you need now, so you will continue to do God's will. Then you will receive all that he has promised."

14 Job 8:7 NLT "And though you started with little, you will end with much."

15 II Corinthians 5:7 NLT "That is why we live by believing and not by seeing."

16 Romans 4:17 NLT "...the God who brings the dead back to life and who brings into existence what didn't exist before."

Scripture Notes

Page 32

17   Proverbs 3:5-6 NLT "Trust in the LORD with all your heart; do not depend on your own understanding. Seeking his will in all you do, and he will direct your path."

18   Hebrews 11:1 NLT "...It is the confident assurance that what we hope for is going to happen. It is the evidence of things we cannot see."

19   Isaiah 55:11 NLT "It is the same with my word. I send it out, and it always produces fruit. It will accomplish all I want it to, and it will prosper everywhere I send it."

20   Jeremiah 29:11 NLT "'For I know the plans I have for you,' says the LORD. 'They are plans for good and not for disaster, to give you a future and a hope."

21   Matthew 19:26 NLT "...Humanly speaking, it is impossible. But with God everything is possible."

22   Romans 8:39 NLT "...nothing in all creation, will ever be able to separate us from the love of God..."

23   Philippians 4:11, 13 NLT "...for I have learned how to get along happily whether I have much or little." "For I can do everything with the help of Christ who gives me the strength I need."

Chapter Three: Experiencing God
Page 47

24   I Samuel 16:7 NLT "...People judge by outward appearance, but the LORD looks at a person's thoughts and intentions."

25   Psalms 37:4 NLT "Take delight in the LORD, and he will give you your heart's desires."

26   See #18

27   See #19

John 15:7 NLT "But if you stay joined to me and my words remain in you, you may ask any request you like, and it will be granted!"

28   Ephesians 3:20 NLT "Now glory be to God! By his mighty power at work within us, he is able to accomplish infinitely more than we would dare to ask or hope."

29   II Corinthians 4:15 NLT "All of these things are for your benefit. And as God's grace brings more and more people to Christ, there will be great thanksgiving, and God will receive more and more glory."

30   Numbers 23:19 NLT "God is not a man, that he should lie. He is not a human, that he should change his mind. Has he ever spoken and failed to act? Has he ever promised and not carried it through?"

31   Matthew 9:29 NLT "Then he touched their eyes and said, 'Because of your faith, it will happen.'"

Scripture Notes

Page 48

32 Romans 8:27 NLT "And the Father who knows all hearts knows what the Spirit is saying, for the Spirit pleads for us believers in harmony with God's own will."

33 Jeremiah 29:12-13 NLT "In those days when you pray, I will listen. If you look for me in earnest, you will find me when you seek me.'"

34 Philippians 4:6-7 NLT " Don't worry about anything: instead, pray about everything. Tell God what you need, and thank Him for all he has done. If you do this, you still experience God's peace, which is far more wonderful than the human mind, can understand. His peace will guard your hearts and minds as you live in Christ Jesus."

35 See #26

36 Psalms 66:10, 12 NLT "You have tested us, O God; you have purified us like silver melted in a crucible." "...We went through fire and flood. But you brought us to a place of great abundance."

Chapter Four: Two-Steppin' with God
Page 61

37 I Timothy 6:12 NLT "Fight the good fight for what we believe…"

38 Job 10:12 NLT "You gave me life and showed me your unfailing love. My life was preserved by your care."

39 Psalms 91:1-2 NLT "Those who live in the shelter of the Most High will rest in the shadow of the Almighty. This I declare of the LORD: He alone is my refuge, my place of safety; he is my God, and I am trusting him."

40 Isaiah 43:2 NLT "When you go through deep waters and great trouble, I will be with you. When you go through rivers of difficulty, you will not drown. When you walk through the fire of oppression, you will not be burned up, the flames will not consume you."

41 Psalms 23:4 NLT "Even when I walk through the dark valley of death,*⁺ I will not be afraid, for you are close beside me. Your rod and your staff protect and comfort me."

42 Psalms 119:105 NLT "Your word is a lamp for my feet and a light for my path."

Page 62

43 Matthew 11:30 NLT "For my yoke fits perfectly, and the burden I give you is light."

44 Psalms 16:11 NLT "You will show me the way of life, granting me the joy of your presence and the pleasures of living with you forever."

45 Proverbs 14:30 NLT "A relaxed attitude lengthens life…"

46 See #23

47 Psalms 23:2-3 NLT "He lets me rest in green meadows; he leads me beside peaceful streams. He renews my strength…"

48 Philippians 1:6 NLT "And I am sure that God, who began the good work within you, will continue his work until it is finally finished…"

49 Ephesians 5:2 NLT "Live a life filled with love for others, following the example of Christ…"

Scripture Notes

50 See #3

51 See #34

52 John 10:10 NLT "...My purpose is to give life in all its fullness."
John 14:6 NLT "...I am the way, the truth, and the life..."

References

Experiencing God: Knowing and Doing the Will of God.
Blackaby, Henry T. & Claude V. King.
LifeWay Press. Nashville, Tennessee: 1990.

Holy Bible: New Living Translation.
Tyndale House Publishers. Wheaton, Illinois: 1996.

Spiritual Renewal Bible: New Living Translations.
House Publishers. Wheaton, Illinois: 1998.

The Open Bible, Holy Bible: New Living Translation.
Thomas Nelson Publishers. Nashville, Tennessee: 1998.

Footnotes

[1] Or *We love him;* Greek reads *We love.*

[2] Some manuscripts read *And we know that everything works together.*

[3] Hebrew *chariots and horses.*

[4] Or *the darkest valley.*

Appreciation Page

If it wasn't for assistance, guidance and a support system I could not have completed or even began this project. From the time it was spoken of, up to the time (finally!) where it's something tangible for readers to experience, I want to take the time to say, "THANK YOU" to:

My parents: Stanley and Felicia Roberts; my siblings: Teesh, Stan, Benny, Dest, and Jamal; my niece and nephew: Naeem and Makkah, my Pastors: Apostle Lesley Ford and Pastor Rosella Ford, Pastor Melvin Miller (editor) & family, Craig Ruhland (typesetter, assist. copyediting, references), Amy Schneider (Evil Genius Design), Marsha Carter (stylist and sponsor) & family, Tameka Jones (make up), ProEx (pictures), Bishop Virgil D. Patterson, Dr. Dorthy Easton (mentor) Amanda Chapman & family, my cousin Hadiyah ("sidekick"), Aunt Valerie ("writing coach"), Grandma Gladys and the rest of my family, Maya Beecham ("writing buddy"), Tiphinie and Dyami King, Tenisha and Damond Hollie and family, Andrae Rainey (referrals, "jakes"), Jenaya Myvett, Reverend Gloria Creighton, Reverend Peggy Elliot, Dawn Shannon (Women of Destiny: Women Born to Write), Minister Sara Shannon, Mary Jo Winston, John and Jaa Avaloz, Akina Carothers & family, Cori Beecham, Sumner Benton, Riley Family, Melissa Logan, Jerome Graham, Arlene Vann, Terry Amos, Deborah Raby & family, Nadira Baijnath, Wayne Howard, Yolanda Holcomb, Collins Family, Bunkers Family, The Maziques, Lyrical Images and Vibin Collective…

And for the many other name(s) that I have probably forgotten to mention, please forgive me, it was not intentional. There is no rank in my love and appreciation for you.

Thank you for all of your support. Thank you for sharing this experience and the vision. Thank you for your encouragement and prayers. You have been a positive motivating force, and an inspiration. Thank you for your diligence and compassion in helping to produce the book's best quality. Thank you for your cooperation and sacrifices of your time, money and energy. No matter who you are, and the size of the role you played, I thank God for you. God bless.

Daily

My grandmother's face is gone
Needing to carry on
Daily more I choose to love
Choosing to live in Harmon-y
Like mother Mary
Harmon to Harmony
Who left a legacy
For me, to follow
The same feet
Through God
Being all that I can be
Daily more I choose to live
To breathe
Living to my fullest potentiality
It takes time
Says the clock
Knowing when to stop
To reflect
And rejuvenate
Making sure
I'm only delivering
What I can take
My fears I meet face to face
My tears are awake
My years in soul
Is flowing age to age
And how I miss
Her lovely face
To feel her warm embrace
To hear her smiley face
To take back those yesterdays
That she might be here in place
Seeing me through
The eyes of destiny
Destined for me to be a queen
Virtuous woman
In faith walking
Still following her foot steps
And through God
Being all that I can be
Doing all that I know how to

Agape love showing through
Puzzles in life
I'm still piecing
Life matching
The form of tapestry
And I'm asking God,
"How can this be?"
Daily I choose life
Liberation of soul
I'm still reaching
To make some impacting
That my God will be pleased
Angels watching over me
God shows His grace and mercies
Tough times are testing
Testing me is strengthening
In all above
Showing me
What I'm truly made of...
Daily as I reflect
On how I'm blessed
I see opportunities
Bits and pieces
Of warm virtue
Vanishing of fears
Developing of confidence
Her face
The lion roars within me
How valuable I am
She still shows me
In God's eyes
It was time for her to leave
To be free in peace, with wings
Carried to Grace and Glory
In her I still believe
And still hear
What she was saying
Daily I choose
In loving memory
Living in Harmony
To live, love, be free
Through God
Being all that I can be
Daily